WITNESSES

WITNESSES

Hoyt Rogers

Spuyten Duyvil
New York City

Witnesses was originally printed by Editora Corripio of Santo Domingo in 1986, as a sample of its proficiency in setting English-language texts; the austere booklet was not intended for general circulation, and has remained largely unavailable.

This first fully-fledged edition of *Witnesses* is published by Spuyten Duyvil, a multicultural press based in New York City. The volume faithfully reproduces the texts from the early chapbook. For permissions and further information, please consult: spuytenduyvil.net I would like to express my gratitude to Gigi Bon and Nati Brand for embarking me on this Venetian voyage, in preparation since 2011.

In altered forms or in translation, many of these poems have appeared in periodicals over the years, including *The Literary Review, Isla Abierta, The International Poetry Review, Antioch Review, The Seagull Catalogue, Plume Poetry,* and *The Fortnightly Review.* I owe a debt of thanks to my editors in various countries for their lasting commitment to poetry.

— HR

Cover Photographs:
The Triton's Trumpet, old and new;
both pictures by Artemisia Vento.

Book and cover design: John Blankwill, in memoriam.

For other books by the author,
please visit hoytrogers.com.

CONTENTS

Preface   7
Their words were lifted ...   17

ARCHIPELAGO

Daybreak   21
The Island   22
Fragments of a Fiction   26
The Well of Light   31
Words from the Sea   37
Four Languages   42
Twilight on the Roof   48

THREE PRAYERS AND A HYMN

And so these miracles...   51
This is the dream...   53
There is no secret...   57
You returned with us...   60

LIVES OF THE SAINTS

Memories   63
Paragraphs   66
Passages   69
The Clouds, The Lake   72
Mirrors   74
The Sermon on the Air   78
Paradise   80
Recessional   83
The Window   87

Our seeing changes us...   89

A BRIEF PREFACE

When *Witnesses* was printed as an informal chapbook in 1986, I handed it out to a small number of friends, and they read it with their customary kindness. Paul Auster said he detected echoes of Hölderlin, while Siri Hustvedt remarked on 'a deep sense of home.' Nicholas Callaway surmised a novel underlying the poems, which would someday rise to the surface (see my *Caribbean Trilogy*). During our stay in Yosemite, Mary Oppen called them 'serious work, heading towards another destination.' Friedhelm Kemp translated the last piece in the book into German, and Nelson Minaya rendered an entire sequence into Spanish. Roselle and William Davenport, along with their daughter Anne, surprised me by learning some passages by heart. The cellist Annette Costanzi organized a reading from the collection in Cairo. Later, Alastair Reid would profess a particular liking for the fragments in prose, and Daniel Lawless would invite me to record a poem for his audio archive on the internet. These generous reactions from writers and artists encouraged me to continue my quest, even though a long hiatus would intervene.

Thirty-nine years on, I can readily comprehend why one literary acquaintance wryly qualified *Witnesses* as 'a bit ecclesiastical.' Such words as 'sin,' 'prayer,' 'saints,' and above all, 'God,' struck him as discordant with contemporary poetry. Though I was puzzled by his comments then, I soon recognized that in the light of prevailing norms, he was right. Having been raised by late Victorians in the rural American South, where polite theological debates about Protestantism,

Catholicism, and Judaism were commonplace, I had absorbed the vocabulary of an earlier era. After that, as a university student for more than a decade on both sides of the Atlantic, I had pored intently over ancient, medieval, Renaissance, and Baroque texts, which had steeped me even further in the mentality of bygone centuries. In addition, from early adolescence onward, I had wandered from region to region, country to country, continent to continent, language to language, with no fixed 'cultural address.' Without fully realizing it, I had composed my poems outside any discernable idiom, time, or place.

To heighten the anomaly, in *Witnesses* I had shifted certain terms away from their current connotations—as attached to an established religion, often bigoted and oppressive. By 'sin,' for example, I meant the Greek 'hamartia'—a 'missing of the mark'—for which the English word is a fateful mistranslation. The original definition brings us nearer to the Buddhist emphasis on eschewing judgments of 'good and evil': we should merely try to pursue what is helpful, rather than what is not. Similarly, terms like 'guilt' and 'fault' echo St. Augustine's concept of 'felix culpa,' the 'fortunate mistake' that leads us to enlightenment. Since I often benefitted from silent retreats in both Trappist monasteries and Vipassana centers, 'prayer' broadly denotes meditation—one variant of which is the writing of poetry. The 'saints' I single out follow Heidegger's 'arduous path of appearance,' and they witness to each other as they explore its complex byways. Suddenly they may stare at us from a painting, like believers before an empty tomb. But what of 'God,' to modern readers the most jarring word of all?

That universal consciousness is invoked only once, at the end of a nightmare about 'the cruelty of grace': the phrase is a willful paradox, linking plenitude to an acceptance of dearth. Recovering the buried roots of another term, 'incarnation' can be imagined as the mind fusing with the body, not trying vainly to transcend it. Our attunement to our surroundings parallels the awareness enjoined by non-Western teachings. Immersion in phenomena takes us outside the self, dispelling the specious duality of subject and object. Just as the watcher becomes the watched, the speaker becomes the spoken. Reconciling the inner with the outer, we are finally at one with language. In those crucial moments, poetry allows us to approach 'the real that we confront,' in George Oppen's words. Such an intensity is never easy to withstand, since it must balance presence and absence in equal measure. Attention to life means mindfulness of death, the natural climax of every process of growth. The altar of art reveals its value only when we abandon it: poetry forces us to grasp that 'the world' is also 'the worldless.'

I am alluding to a book by William Bronk—along with Oppen, the Anglophone poet of recent times who most lucidly dispensed with verbal pyrotechnics. The above paragraph may sound severe, but I consider it an unvarnished statement of things as they are. Running counter to some of the terminology in *Witnesses*, I was always 'heading towards another destination': the primacy of the here and now. As I have transformed these nostalgic early poems into other poems, (compare my recent book, *Thresholds*), I have shed many of their wistful illusions, though I would never disown their fundamental stance. In his memoir of the first phase of his life, James Merrill referred to his youthful avatar as 'a different person.' Certainly, the reader I am today can still recognize my less experienced self as a fellow traveler, even as a shy and awkward younger brother. The fact that I have radically rewritten many of these pieces several times suggests that for me at least, they contain 'an unbreakable kernel of truth.' In poetry, all we can do is approximate our core intentions as humbly as possible, realigning the signposts as we hasten to Samarra.

Looking back at these poems from decades ago, despite my impression of composing them outside time and place, I can see how they join America, Europe, Africa, and Asia to the Hispanic Antilles— my perennial winter refuge. Owing to a lifelong fascination with Italy, that other touchstone, where my weeks and months have turned into years, this book has been reborn in Venice. Once we penetrate its secrets, this is the city where we can most vividly play our part in the theatre of memory, repeating our predetermined lines. Though water-worlds are essentially one—with their tides, storms, and tranquil reflections—the sea of *Witnesses* is not the Adriatic, but the Caribbean. Against that tropical radiance, other backdrops hover as mirages: the Arctic wilderness, the French Alps, the Carolina countryside, a temple in Kyoto, the glass monadnocks of New York. Like castaways, we fold our pages and slip them into a bottle; those who find them on another shore must make of them what they will. As we write, read, and remember from island to island, the ocean that divides us also brings us close.

For
K. R., M. E., L. V.,
M. O., and G. G.

...whereby the dayspring.
Luke 1:78

Your true mind is always with whatever you see.
Shunryu Suzuki

The self is no mystery, the mystery is
That there is something for us to stand on.
George Oppen

Their words were lifted for a moment, like a burden from the sea: love itself which could not say how it balanced, whole, unafraid in the dominant air. Here, she had whispered, with that kindness shadows have, speaking to him now of what she knew, the years when she wandered and the years of her imprisonment. Voices, interrupting, intertwining with our own, broken off where the weather drives them down in ragged clouds, in helpless rain, in the uneven dispensations of the light. The features in the mirror turn and blur, the profiles of the numerous.

We could not understand without a witness, she had said: we were too weak to see the truth. He was thirty, he was forty, it was written in his eyes: but now he wanted it to be his fault. The words grow more forgiving, more forgetful as the meaning falls away from them, takes time with them.

The tree is alone with its branches. The leaves are alone with the wind.

ARCHIPELAGO

DAYBREAK

The circle of morning widens...

Reflection on reflection,
        the waters of the world
open their corolla to the light

The outer edge, the scarfskin
        of the sun, reaches deftly
from the windows to the floor

The sea looks up and seizes you again
        in the even wind of
clarity

        the path
that awakens
        speech

THE ISLAND

1

Jagged pieces thrown
    like scraps of tin
into a sea
    where night, casually dropped
does down to meet them:
    islands, in the window
quickly eclipsed.

But later—
    it seemed years afterward—
riding past the hills
    we could not see from above,
the dim, sudden bays
    glint like gunshot.

2

In the dark the sheets begin,
    the sails,
the coils of rope
    lying calmly on the deck,
your arms tied together
    in the thick, loosened knot
that covers your face.
    The body surrenders—
willing, headless.

The canvas pouring out,
      the slow ripple billowing,
the undertow of skin...
      No motion in the air
but dawn, though sails
      go taut around the mast.

The whale spout, rising
      in the urgent, waveless sea.

3

It was that child again,
      the one who used to sleep
on the latticed summer porch,
      swinging in the cage of air and heat.
The green slats were swaying back and forth,
      the thin shadows inched across the bed.

His arms did not hold you,
      could not.
Cautious, even in sleep
      you were cautions
of the burden, which at dawn
      would disappear again, like sleep.

4

The goat trail crumbled into red along the hill.
Words, a death that survives us
under the skin of things,
the landscape more than apparent.

Climbing to the cliff
where the fort stood, low
masonry pitted by the light—
it was like walking
on the fierce blankness of the sea,
blue, at noon,
another sky below the sky.

A boat fastened the horizon,
rocking with the wide,
white metric of its sails.
The rhythm blinded,
turning inside out,
out further.

5

Below the fronds of mottled color,
ragged blue and bottle green,
trunks of coral grow,
patient and unmoved,
in the necessary light:
ventricles and valves,
though the tide pulls through them,
hardened.

But now there is only a sense
of the familiar, the invisible...
waves, along the reef,
that never reach the shore;
they break on hidden walls,
and the foam leaps in circles,
lapsing, repeated.
In the distance, out to sea,
there is nothing—nothing we have known
can still occur.
That is why the heart
does not fail us.

FRAGMENTS OF A FICTION

Far afield—only wind

        the rise and sag
           strung out

    an entryway—

As though the splendor
        were in this:

    that you
mean nothing to me

           ★ ★ ★

The river almost stilled
        the water flooded
           with reflections
    sleeping
        on the surface

    an interval

           its absence
        slowly fills

as sleep
               gives way to other space
and speech of birds
               becomes
                              a shelter
        for desire

★ ★ ★

Surfacing

                       an eyeless bronze
        all surface

                              like the sea
               from a distance

                                       a cliff

               both of us

        unreachable

★ ★ ★

The houses crystallize
                       square as salt
        their gardens presuppose
               a mineral fact

        Weeds   along the wall
                              huddle

drying in the sun
headless   stuck like needles
in the rock
pricking the light with their shadows

But at noon:
an equanimity
a parchment

without a text

★ ★ ★

A stone

as it happens
to rest

on another

★ ★ ★

And beautiful...

though later
you will sit somewhere
being old
in clumsy shoes

reminiscent

humbled

★ ★ ★

The angelfish
that dart away along the reef

                        Time
    blindly
                groping after them

                ★ ★ ★

And as though I could save you—

                you call out my name
        over and over

                The names will change—
        the seasons
                        the weather

                ★ ★ ★

Faint reflections
        on the floor:

                starlight, shielded
                        the thinnest edge
        of suns

                        and still it cuts us

                even our flesh
        indefinite

                ★ ★ ★

"I write you for the last time—
                    not knowing who you are—
                                        not caring

        Love:
    when we say that, it is
                        a word

            Near or distant

                        we will always be that single force
    of happiness"

                        ★ ★ ★

"It is this love—

            which is too great

            and therefore
                    will be forgiven—

                only this love
        which allows me to   write—

                                to speak

            from this page

                        where I am still

THE WELL OF LIGHT

1

The palms on the harbor sandbar
     almost growing from the sea—
their miracle refused
     by the lighthouse, the drowsy ships,
the tired evidence of noon.

Islands, too clear in the sudden light,
     as though a hand had lifted the curtain—
but it was only the wind behind the wind,
     the impenetrable walls of clarity.

2

The house shuts down on itself
     wall after wall to enclose
the eye of light, the gleaming well;
     voiceless, the heart of day,
to which we must give voice.

There is no impulse now,
     no backward and no forward...
the listless swaying of the fronds,
     the house, the city lapsing
like a sea without a shore,
     without finality.

3

The odd assortments in this room,
        as though jumbled from a suitcase.
The scraps of time badly pasted
        into a day, another day.

Sickened, in these tropics,
        a memory of geese
flying through the northern night,
        their disconsolate cries
bringing them further, south.

4

The pebbles on the beach,
        for the first time perfected,
pale and cold. This was a world
        in which the slightest move
would be negated. The sunlight slipping
        down the wall, the coming night
which the stars would keep awake
        were like terms in an equation.

Five in the afternoon. The others could believe
        in where they had to go,
what they had to suffer,
        who might save them.
The footsteps of children
        running in the street, their voices
raw with expectancy.

5

A tingle in the air
        but not a chill,
here where summer follows summer.
        Leaves green and drop
in constant rounds
        of disappearance and return.

The body, passive
        in impassive hands, a misplaced
object. The book was reading it,
        the room had left it behind
in deliberate degrees,
        a weightlessness,
a breathing.

6

The city deserted, the sun
        still at bay.
Unseemly, the quietness:
        as though this morning
were the first,
        the only.

Hidden in a courtyard
        blocks away, a rooster crows
in someone else's childhood—
        though I am the one
who remembers.
        That cry tears the calm
of the garden here. Remember:
        the door is open.
There is no house.

7

Here he could sleep;
        it would be his grave
of sleep. The blinding drizzle of noon,
        the wind fanning out in the palms:
memorial
        of all that is.

He had thought that his fortune
        was the past
and found
        no sequel
            now, no burden—

        Time
raining down on his face,
        he wept
in the infinite light.

8

The white walls
        empty of grief
and the regular bricks
        cool underfoot—

The humble planes and squares
        of barely furnished rooms:
some law must rule us,
        even here.

But the body
        with its valves
and gaskets—
        though the stars
revolve to wider arcs—

        dawns as they race
in a fever
        from the sun
and rustles with the weather,
        leaf against leaf.

9

A gust of wind through the stems
        and they vibrate at the window,
dilating greener. The heartbeat
        quickens in this moment,
but it is not "ours".

        Morning scrabbles through the garden,
through the ground that moves
        like water. Cells ignite
and their music is
        restless, never ending.

WORDS FROM THE SEA

I

The house was still at a distance, a plain just over the hill, in the wide horizontals of sleep. The echo of that dream kept retreating through the chambers of the shell, the recesses smaller and smaller.

He could say: the cup, the chair, and the voices within him were silenced. But now the words would fail him, too much his own. Awake again, he listened to the church bells, the traffic, the songs on the radio next door, muffled by the droning of the fronds. Here he was encircled, no return. Now, at last:

This was the only place he could be found.

2

Followed from the roof, the cruise ships
    head for port, pennants fluttering
beneath the stars; and will diminish
    what they praise: arrival
from the sea and the homeless dark.

That harbor is not ours, the ransom of the world
    transformed into our words—
fire alive in the ashes, blown
    beyond the threshold, light
only theirs. And this must mean

they turn against us
    because they too are things,
left to lead us on;
    or lead us back
to the time
    always before us.

3

At twilight the facade began to drift, as light as wood. The
Virgin, carved in stone above the door, had been delivered
from the rock; now she balanced on the wind like a figure-
head, urging the nave out to sea. He stood for a moment in
that flickering, the unsure refuge of what the words could
save. Their faces were turned away, manifold as leaves in eve-
ning prayer. Reproofs and thanks, gains and losses circling
back to end in simple departure: the stones, the words, the
unsure refuge.

4

Shadowless, the hollows of the eyes in this paradise,
    the blessed isle returning to the sun.
And later: deadening the night, the stars intensify,
    their brilliance close to the unnatural.

"Romantic," they will say, and yet we know
    it is the distance we are taking
that possesses us, and thus it is
    that distance we possess.
A plainness, nothing more: the crescent moon,
    lying flat as it approaches with the tide,
a shallow boat, bare and illumined.
    The fragile hull,
resting on the sea for an instant,
    lifts it into clarity, into desire:
the ocean floor rises in the mind—
    there is no secret now,
no shelter from the light.

Here the summer is a constant
    and the words of that summer are as real
as the details of the reef,
    the bright particulars of love—
which are closest to death, they have said,
    even closer than the words.

5

You told about their travels, the life they spent collecting things, and how their house burned down one night, "an utter loss." This morning I think of that house—hearing the birds abandon their calls, like ashes floating up on the clear heat of day.

Words, patient and sure...You wrote that they could save, not the earth or even ourselves; but the remnants of our hope, a feeble radiance, unsealed as from a stone. The alter of that light will make us worthy to say the common names—which shield us, as though time were not indifferent.

I knew you old in the mastery of exile, of horses and of sails; older still in the language of clarity, and of respect. There was the vision of the woman you found sleeping on the beach. The war and the dying in the war, the horror of the world we must believe, because it is impossible. Belief, more than they—or we—have had in songs.

We are left to mean this life again, alone. But because we are speaking of the facts, we know that they can never be recounted. Reliving them a thousand times would still not be enough—not to face them or get behind them, but even to see the surface. There are things that never register. There are words we cannot file away.

6

He had not come to beginning
        or end. But now he knew
that every silence
        would also be a language,
would carry in itself
        the form, the courage of a language.

        Blindness . . . shining out.

By broken curbs,
        or on stairs littered with glass
he had stopped, still
        as light, straining
to hear these words, but hears
        the world.

FOUR LANGUAGES

I FALL

The principle was ruin
        hardened into form, failure so severe
it had been realized

        not even to discuss it, at least
to pretend you are all right
        assuming we can leave tomorrow

that is why we could not look you in the eyes
        would say it came from nowhere

        window
of precision turned away from the household
        gods, in the end merely creatures
of a history   and watch with us, see out
        of us beyond the walls
the suburbs racing to the white broken
        line where he had fallen
straight to the water   not what he had promised
        to the fathers, brilliance of artifice,
wings   only his body had suffered
        bare as the falling

line of that weight   lowered to the sea
        string plucked beside the cliff
still visible sound

2 PROCESS

Depth of a dizziness, depth
  of those voices lowered to the sea,
curves of their movement
  rolling as a lightness in the half-dark
language of the whales

  and it glistened, spiraled, shot out
into the night   the fragments still conscious
  though nothing was altered

admitting we have wanderedour happiness
  lived in the unknown
at some point   is terror

  still unused to this instrument, speak
only one of those voices and lowered to the sea
  how long to rise again unowned, speak

flickered blinding on the page to gravitate in
  memory, heaven nor hell neither transferred
nor explicable creature of a voice
  turning, lost in the folds

refuse to believe you
  that being, any being in the first
motion of its cells
  is already in torture

the creature cannot represent
            the world cannot
represent

            power that jettisons
intricate waste of intricate
            light   process   light
dimming to begin again

            and hear us somewhere
hear us from this speech

3 PASSAGE

Passage of the currents, shifting
    migration through the sea
birds veering in patterns
    slow erosion of the earth

passage of the breezes through the grass
    on low hills, wandering
to small deaths
    unnoticed

imagine we are heard, refused—
    particles of history   the fables
swept away with us
    no need to have constructed
the tangle of knowledge and desire
    to end with the current, exhaustion
and ticking down—
    machinery to rust
in a field under sun and no part
    of it salvaged

        nor even
light   immense   disaster
    of their bodies, lifted and torn in
the wrecked stillness of love

       retreating now the more it comes forward
the more we have approached
         union with the world   touching
it and straining at its surfaces   the mind
         has also suffered like a body

rolled back
       in that avalanche

cry
       above the passage
heavier than rock

4 MIRAGE

Valley of dust   of eclipse
      in the thunder of dryness
river running dry   stricken dumb

      remote   the procession of the clouds
buried like a phrase
     the mind has also suffered

     The wind on our faces
driving us to thirst   as though a wind
      on the face of the waters
the whole morning lashed
      by the winter sea

 unanswerable unanswerable
"without whom the world would crumble"

      wild   in the light of the storm
now   where the invisible

      the rain that slaps the sidewalks, the trees
the words that are rags
      the lizards skittering   the flies
now
      where as though
in a sunburst   through the clouds
      a mountain   green or blue
as though a voice
      and lifted from the sea
shudders with the light of noon
      scattering reflections on the waves

TWILIGHT ON THE ROOF

The evening light rides the clouds
        to the horizon; their branches
sprout and break at the tips
        in the unlivable   yet gentle
blue

        The sun leaves a stain
of faint and wordless meaning
        on the pages we have shut,
pressing the day for darkness   though it

        lies further out, a leaden hull
listing to the west below the afterglow of sex
        still suffused in the feathery heights,
in their tumbling manes

        They canter homeward to Hesperides,
the uncharted ocean laps at their hooves
        and their nerves rebound
to the salty gunsmoke of freedom, the silver
        roar that fades and blackens
to spare us for the night within the night

THREE PRAYERS AND A HYMN

And so these miracles, you said, as the years draw to an end.

The changes in temperature the last few days have been like
a restless dilation, an ominous breathing of the elements.
Sometimes I imagine those pure, empty latitudes where
winds scour and buffet the surface of the sea, where there is
no one for hundreds of miles to watch the rising or setting
of the sun.

This morning I read of a terrible incident. A young man had
been flown with six months of supplies into a remote region
of Alaska, but had made no provision for his return. As winter
approached he began to starve, competing with the wolves
for a few stray rats and meager scraps from gutted carcasses.
Finally, unable to continue any longer, he killed himself with
his rifle, commending his soul to God. He had come almost
in reverence to photograph the spring, the rapid summer of
a wilderness unknown as yet to man. His diary, found beside
the frozen corpse, tells of green awakenings in isolated woods,
in a valley without a name, beside a lake that is also nameless,
unpossessed even by the labels of our speech. We can only
guess the loneliness that he endured as his confidence gave
way before the truth, the brutal coldness of a landscape he
had loved for its innocence—the absence of human nearness,
human stain. And there was none: no one to hear his final
words or touch him in the gray October light. Was he fearless,
even then? His journal would lead us to think so. It is moving,
his insistence on keeping that record down to the last few
hours before his death. Of his suicide, planned for days, he
says simply that he knows it will not hurt—as though he had
conquered, if only for the interval of those brief words, the
horror of man before the density of things, the ruthless silence
that stands outside ourselves.

If we pause at the brink, we are lost in the abyss. But the stronger we are, the more we are sheltered; where danger is, salvation also grows. We cannot save ourselves, only the witness can; and we are witnesses to others—but more often, to ourselves. This is history, this is the moment, this is the future I foretell. That witness is radically different, radically one: our past, present, and future speak out of that voice, which we answer only as echo. Still it is our witness that refracts in the impersonal—our one leap to freedom as we plunge into nameless waters, the unknowable abyss, now named, now known.

How we stumble at that threshold, weak as our belief; how the blood surges up and erupts from the mouth in a keenness of deliverance. The blank, impassive eyes of the creature we confront cannot recognize our face, cannot see any shadow or light. Our death is purified by his unconsciousness: nothing but our own personal cry that doubles back to anonymity. What line divides us from him now? The winds on the sea are no less than we, because we have become no more than they.

I would speak of a perpetual erosion, the sediment of living in this world that settles in our hearts, insofar as we consent to be the heart of things. It is our only elevation, final grace; as though, on a stage, the acting were suddenly the real. The birds that hiss and whistle in the dead, sapless tree are the same as the glare flashing hard between two paragraphs of rain, and are the same as our words as they form on the page, quickly, irresistibly, the sign that they have never been our own. We relinquish one another, we abandon even ourselves, and a seething, rustling field of expectant air opens up in the place and the time where we have been. What we have not said, what we have not and never will say and which is all a singing, a silence. . .

★   ★

★

This is the dream I will remember all my life; the dream that never returned, but to which I always return.

It began as a nightmare, a desperate chase through narrow alleyways in a deserted modern city, past block after block of concrete and dingy brick. He was pursuing me with the coolness and skill of a sure-footed predator, confident of his prey. Why he wanted to kill me I did not know: all I knew was that his powerful tread brought him closer with every bound, and that time was running out. I tried to cry for help, but my shouts were stifled in my throat before they could form. No one could help me now, in any event; no one would dare oppose that savage force, the athletic spring forward of the panther to the kill.

At last we emerged on a large, asphalted square—a parking lot, abandoned long before. Sheer brick walls hedged it in on every side, but at the far corner I saw a door, my only hope of escape. My lungs were bursting from the race, my whole body throbbing with pain. In a final surge of energy I bolted towards the door and flung it back in his face. Exhausted, I lunged up the stairs, although I knew there was no use in going on; I was no longer running toward freedom, but toward death. We climbed for what seemed like an hour. The rhythm of our feet, pounding on metal steps, reverberated loudly in the stairwell of scarred cement.

We reached the top, and now he was so close I could feel his breath on the nape of my neck. His breathing was even, self-assured. I rushed to the edge of the roof: but here there was no escape, unless by falling hundreds of feet to the pavement far below. Leaning against a low concrete wall, I turned to face him, paralyzed by fear. I would reason with him, I would make him realize that there was no earthly purpose in destroying me. Wildly I clung to these final absurdities— though looking into his eyes, I readily perceived the uselessness of words. His eyes were the palest of blues, unblinking and expressionless, opaque and inhuman as a shark's. His thick black hair was cut in a style oddly antique, as though he had lived decades earlier. It was impossible to tell how old he was, whether sixteen or thirty-six. But aside from that strange absence in his stare, what struck me most was his ease in chasing me down. His polar-white, flawless skin did not betray the slightest sign of exertion: no rush of blood to the surface, no trace of the sweat in which I was drenched. He stood there as though he had merely been waiting—calmly and patiently waiting for me to come. Now he held a revolver which at some point, in the way of dreams, had materialized out of no-where. It was the only bridge between us: he held it perfectly still in his strong, steady hand, resting the tip of the barrel against my chest.

This is the part of the dream to which I constantly return. I stood there for many minutes, gazing straight into his eyes. They were near, very near, but endlessly remote, lost in a mad-ness as immovable as rock. It could never be his fault, as it could never be the fault of the world, of the streets or the walls, the sunlight or the air, that I must die at such and such an hour, in such and such a place. He did not see me, but I saw him, saw him clearly. He was merciless, immobile and serene, a marauder in the sea poised to strike, an angel with his sword unsheathed, pausing to observe the spectacle of time. The same serenity began to settle over me, enfold me in its silence more and more. I was floating gently upward through the clearing well of sleep. The end of what I thought of as myself was un-avoidable—was close with the closeness of a love. Nor could I have asked for any change, in this or any passage of that dream. I would not wake as one does from a nightmare, just at the point of dying; I would live my death, live it to the fullest, be-fore emerging to the light of another day.

He pulls the trigger now. The bullet is slow to enter my chest, slow to part the waters of my blood. They stand on either side, a canyon of red, a fathomless trench in an ocean teeming with life, the frenzy of reproduction, hidden couplings, the primal beginnings of the earth. Slowly the bullet explodes and splinters my bones one by one, the chest heaves and tilts like a sinking ship, the rib cage caving inward, rolling down and back in a long, prickly surge, the blood gushing out in a salty exhalation, warm and red, flowering deeply rooted from the belly to the mouth, spilling from the lips and running in waves toward the calm unflinching eyes of the horizon, pale and blue, retreating to the end of all that is, the seething, vibrating curve of the possible, impossible. Blood of my body, which was given up for you. And you know in this moment, which will last as long as you live, that there is only again and again the ritual of death, the flood of desire in willing sacrifice, the lover's cruelty, the mineral tenderness of God, slowly, slowly wrenching us out of ourselves to the word forever unspoken, beyond our being, the kind, blissful radiance of nothingness and prayer.

There is no secret in the end. The objects and occurrences rest in simple clarity as on a table, and even their shadows are luminous. The transparence is the mystery itself: as might be suddenly a place that we have known for many years, a place so familiar we had pictured it from memory without a fault. But what of it now...and now again? I would watch those things and places and events as they swim down a river of change and I would say: yes, there is that change and it is constant, it is ruthless. But the clarity is only that the change was not withheld, that the things and places and events were present from the first in their causes, their increase and decline, their prolongation in the world eternally to come, like fossils in the peaks of young, still thrusting mountains. Having been so close to death, so certain of death, in that landslide by the glacier long ago, I had learned that all my history was happening at once, had learned to see that every face is always various and one: the fragile glances of the child already outlined by old age; the middle years suspended like a trail along the ridge, awash with noon and four directions of the wind; the thinning vision of the old almost delivered from the past, fresher than the child's in second innocence, the whitening forgetfulness of dawn.

The run-off issued from a cave below the point where massive, frozen slabs sheared off and crashed against the rocks. I cannot give the explanation. The glacier, bearing down on the thick vaults of ice above the stream, made them glow, intently blue, an inner life: a shining life as far apart from us, as separate as our own. I have the photographs, the negatives gone brittle with the years. Partial and confused, like sight itself they are a way we have of writing with the light. As though our fictions could be real, we believe that every moment forms a stratum in our earth. green, blue, and white, the blurred striations tilt away from us, retreating inch by inch, hour by hour; the fallen sky inside the cave, the clouded green of the water streaked with white, our bodies in their youth as cold and perfect as the ice.

We sleepwalked through that danger, coming home. The boulders only balanced where an avalanche had left them days before. Climbing back, halfway up, the mountain moved. The shifting footholds set us loose in a place outside of place, a fissure in the ground of continuity: the horror of that motion launched a counterforce in time. All of my experience unreeled like lightning in reverse, rushing in an instant from the present through the past, as though I could return beyond my birth. But now there was no backward and no forward, nothing but a seamless band of brightness thrown like cloth into the air, outside of any sequence, beginning or end. Irrational, wild as the world itself, I asked what I had done to deserve an early death. The valley roared around me with the thunder of the fall, the boulders as they slipped and hurtled down the slope, heaving their terrible weight overhead and on every side.

When was it that..? The rumbling was blanketed. Silence. Silence still. In the shelter of the cliff, we were drinking from a spring that trickled out of granite, threading down frayed and broken through the ferns.

The wall of stone, the ferns wedged stubbornly in all its crevices. If you could see it is the rock growing there, the living rock—could read the stone no longer as an enemy, but as a spelling of the testament. I am the rock, I am the water from its side. The water in its newness almost pungent to the tongue, the acrid taste sinking into us like sunlight sinking downward into stone. The particles of flavor sifting deeper, piercing layer after layer, whirring in the quietness, the half-light of the mountains. Half of the valley is day, and half is night. Our path curves between them like a flag as it curves into the wind. The folds overlap and double back, fixed unawares to the axis of our being, to our sin. The imperfection is the mark; the fracture in the glass is the imprint, the name that we are called. The way it shatters is the way we are reclaimed.

We promised you these moments when a plane is passing over or a cock is crowing or a neighbor plays a tune on the harmonica. And who are you if not the one who waits for us to wait, to be still in the moving air of the one creation, the humming, glittering heartlessness of things, through which we are released like a single breath, a single circumstance, a single word... This is what is happening—all that has ever happened or ever will. The game of time only saves us from our suffering, and even from our happiness for now, as burdens that would be too great for us to bear.

The swing behind the plain brick house... My sister was too young then not to know; I pushed her higher and higher, she was breathless with the freedom. She would be thirty if she had not died so long ago, loved, loved and buried in our thoughts, my family's thoughts, these many years.

You returned with us to the grave,
       holding our hands in turn.
You spoke: this was your gesture,
       raised in words. Now our sister
was dead, her face was thin
       and far away behind the film
that had covered her eyes:
       the filters, the blackouts, the sheets.
That morning had seemed like a dream,
       but it was not.
The truth happens once,
       that is the truth.
And wake again to the tender film
       of breath on all the windows of the house.
The dust on the table is her prayer,
       the table set with dust
our morning feast.

Dust, grave and still, o morning light.
       This was the hollow song she sang,
the music to be filled.
       O witness, come.

LIVES OF THE SAINTS

MEMORIES

I

At the center of the room, the ceiling fan rotates like a snow-fall, blanketing the air with its sound. The child I used to be remembers me—as though I were home again, as though it were summer. This was one of our naps on the screened side-porch, in the burning early hours of afternoon. The haze fil-ters brightly through the green wooden blinds, like the glare from the drifts of our sleep.

2

In the stairwell of our sleep, the landings are our memories; the doors that open out from them are dreams.

The quilt arched over you at bedtime like a canopy, a tunnel through the dark. The pieces in the pattern were cut from their old clothes—the aunts, and the uncles, and the cousins; the ones you knew, and the ones you thought you knew. The threads seemed as worn as the wires in the screen, the tiny squares of iron that curled and unraveled into rust.

The house is lost, bewildered by the spring, by the azaleas spilling wildfire through the pines. The picnics there at Easter, and the tables spread with white. Our sister's gloves, not much larger than a doll's; the brittle, crinkled sheen of her organdy dress. The days would grow longer, and the sun would push its way through steam already rising from the ground, the daily immolation of the dew.

The body drops forever like a stone into that stream, drowned by the heat of the hours, dividing their flow.

3

The Shelbys were driving home in the Oldsmobile, poking along as slow as snails, after their morning errands in town. Their only pleasure was in dragging out the slightest task and most trivial thought to its ultimate length, its absolute thinness. Plastic straws, paper cups, even the silver wrappers from sticks of chewing gum were carefully stashed away. You never know what might come in handy, the twists and turns of life are so hard to predict, and you don't want to be caught up short, now, do you?

I suppose you remember Hattie Moe, that old colored woman who lived in a shack and the town council finally had to tear it down it got so filthy, full of rags and junk and thousands of dollars in change. You might of thought somebody would come along and sue for her rights. But them was different times, different people.

Don't you listen to the Shelbys what they say, they ain't no justice in this world. She stood at the corner and rattled on for hours, frozen rain in a broke-down shrine, thanks for the memory. You welcome, anytime. Down the street we got a pawnshop, House o' Laz'rus, where they resurreck your money from the dead.

4

The farm along the Maidendown,
      at nightfall,
when the final light of day,
      the most detached,
pauses on the crown of the tallest tree.

Deep in the slue, a woodpecker
      takes up the beat.
Crows squabble hoarsely
      in distant fields.
Behind the windows of the house,
      nothing moves.
Squirrels forage closer,
      clattering the bone-dry leaves.

Nearer, too,
      the nighthawk with its cry
that blinks on and off.
      Two of them together now, unseen,
but like signals in the dark,
      flashing out of sequence.

PARAGRAPHS

1

I like to hear how things keep silence in the room. The objects are the words that wait in rows, distinct and plain as blades of grass. The blades are really there, their edges filed by the perfect plan, a clarity invading every particle; an undertow, equivalent to each bare facet of the earth. No one can protect us here, in this unwinding from the center and circumference. We feel that wave merely as an energy, but it should be our inmost choice: our happiness, our limitless decease.

2

Everything repeats or is repeated. To her, each sound was familiar, each sound was a cry. "Death, she is welcome, too." The woman who said this was poor and old, sitting with death in her frail wooden house; standing with death at the door, on the concrete steps. The house was clean of the odor: this was a place for the others, inclining around her, off balance in the world where she was balancing. For a while yet they would keep the fragrance from the rooms. But in her heart the ticking radiated outward, soft and tired like the answer from her eyes.

3

Now I will settle back and dream of the fireflies, blameless and mute in the summer leaves and clouds of green. Across the fields they make a runway of forgetfulness, the signals multiply until they drown us in their surf, the pure throb of process. This is "beauty": our perception, even here, is the cannibal of love. We lose ourselves again among the eating and the eaten, the seeing and the seen. We notice, and we notice not to notice. Ending it would not help us. Beginning again, oh yes. Beginning again.

4

From the first salutation by the well to the locking of hands as we vault across the hill, this love of ours sheds so many worlds we would never want to own one—if all we have is time. What a music it has taken to dispel those ancient reveries, and now they leave a new, traceless moment, an absolute desire... As in that memory we walk ahead of other memories, not even waving good-bye, so the shoreline seems indented for our pleasure, the skin just a series of small, good-natured accidents. Invited, inviting, we separate. Here at the foot of the mountain, each of us chooses his path.

5

But in the corner of this tale the first mate weeps, and the captain holds him steady with his gaze. Such are the silences, the hollows and the caves where their watchfulness will germinate. Gently then, so gently. The prow cuts through the deep with a life of its own. The wind unfolds letter after letter, which nobody bothers to read. Now we can truly say we have given it all. Our consent lights the room, fills the dawn as it lifts from the sea and from the land—traveling with other mists, with other brightnesses: distinctions that widen into day.

PASSAGES

I

Every gospel gives us notice. The eviction will be carried out in time, the furniture stacked on the sidewalk. The children will be sent to other schools, and forget they ever knew us. The messenger himself has disappeared. He used to be a boy from our neighborhood. But now, if we saw him on the street, we could not say: he was the one.

The message also vanishes, refracted in the prism of our questioning, our praise. The spectrum will divide and redivide, the truth will be refined and redefined, the crystals feeding on the light—as darkness unifies the world by hiding it.

Remember: this extinction is our place.

2

The frozen banks of whiteness on the shelves, the print flecking page after page like dirt on the snow; the drifts where we foundered on the years, the abscess of years. Beneath the lamps, the letters hung in dormancy like bats; or started from their sleep, but were too old to leave the circuit of the cave.

The blankness still endures behind the stains, the traces of vermin and ink, of water and blood. "I know a way out of hell." But what was that way? Buried in books, far removed on this calm afternoon, the photographs swarm into memory, the faces of the tortured, the dead.

The branches ease into flower. Let them take their time. We thought that we had learned all the rules of despair, how the prisons would spring open on command. Here there are no hints to be revealed. The hillsides stir to fullness without a sound.

3

The lagoon nods in and out, half awake behind the palms. You are still on this island which you love, more attached to the rock than to the sea, to the bedrock underneath the yawning trenches and the foam.

Wild as sudden bird song heard on a busy street, to which the rest is only echo.

At daybreak, the clouds surround the sun like the announcement of a miracle. But they are the miracle themselves, a monument built and abolished. The horizon pales to a color past belief, the color of blindness, inexplicable and unrenewable... True history will never be recorded.

4

The empty one is not to feel the guilt. He lives too deeply in that shade, rooted in his shadow like a tree.

To the north, many autumns will trespass through the woods. But spring sits alone in a single leaf. Before our sentence even finishes, it rings from all the trunks.

The budding twigs are not what they were before.

To stand in that passage may be the most difficult thing. The water ripples hard across our feet—until, in the watchful stream, every pebble clarifies.

The currents flag, trailing back, crawling to a stop. The spiders weave across them like a mirror on a mirror, doubling the surface of the world.

5

The city is restored by evening light, by nothing more; the houses welcome us like harbingers. Their windows realign in the same slender smile, the same horizon.

Where darkness penetrates the day...an act of love...the sky is sea, the sea is sky.

THE CLOUDS, THE LAKE

The words, the rain and thunder of the storm, the jagged strokes of rage were all interior: a cry of the heart, but only that—a crude, relentless cry.

The movement succeeding them now will seem like immobility, just as the clouds appear suspended in the air when the air is as still as the light. We are breathing it, then; the air has lightened us, too. The day becomes so calm that we forget about our aims, and the fatigue of the journey flows away in the thin transparence of the world. Do not break it, we say. The claims of love lose their force as soon as we stop thinking of events and even of intentions as directed toward ourselves. We protest, we refuse, until we learn that leaving the circle is the same as giving in to it. Above our hatred and revolt, the clouds advance across the sky in their predetermined order, their absorption in the parable—which if we follow it, will save us. Predestination is the fire's name for grace: the disguise from the attic we wore once like three thieves will never deceive us again. The afternoon has ebbed to the second line of trees. Because we watch within the shadow, we can see. The slanting sun is also merciless, though milder to the form of things as they are.

Therefore the lake. And we are swimming in the slow procession of the clouds on its darkened glass, a reflection among reflections. The present is already past, the bitterness of love betrayed seems as mute and unassuming as the green of the leaves, the heat of high summer, the stark outcroppings of rock. O heart of stone, if we could love each other now in that silent, hopeless way, stone against stone, light against light... It may be that we have no choice. The water falls away from us to incomprehensible depths, the shore retreats from us more triumphantly than we can know, a farewell, a greeting from the other side where we do not exist, a sign from the dead which we will never read. But that is the spirit in which we are loved, a spirit devoid of the spiritual—loved in the sense of a stillness, an emptiness, loved in the sense of an indifference.

MIRRORS

1 THE GALLERY

They were supposed to be just pictures of the world, diamonds cutting clear through the mind. But within them we retreat, when we ought to be outside them. Here we cannot hide from what we know.

The process of ruin is so slow, we hardly believe it is our home. The mirror frames us under glass, and we change sides with the image, back and forth.

The naked trees whisper there of greenery. The early flowers bend and shiver near a brook. Seated on the ground, the mother holds her son in a simplicity of grief—not grief, only suspension, as the sky would hold a cloud.

The flesh surrenders gratefully, unfurling like a flag, without a genesis. A moment in our curve back to earth; a spot along the path softly grassed: the path as one.

The ocean crowds against our shorelines, both the sung and the unsung, with all the mourning and the luster of a voice.

2 PEARLS

Lustful, lustrous. Words tease and play, link in pairs related only by their sound. The fish swim upstream into their element—coupled, killed.

"What's to complain?" She said it with a Yiddish intonation. "Practice your atonement: use the best plates every day."

That is why she clung to them, the chosen ones, though she was born beneath the hail, the star of the sea. After all, details have to be what saints like most.

From the Himalayan pass, she wandered back where she began. Falling flat on her face, breaking her nose. A crucifix, discarded in the snow.

The soul descends, descends, but its descent will live forever, incorruptible. Forgiveness will be hers, because she loved.

Now she slumps computing in the dovecote of New York, the stable of prophecy, to educate mankind. "Underlings! If this is dead, what isn't?"

The answer thrones and towers from the evidence, blinking through the night with a million proofs. Under scales of shiny glass, the human masters coil inside their artifice, make love, and go to sleep.

Redemption day will blast them to eternity, each and every cell: the absolute division of heresy and truth. But for now, emptied drink cans line the room. Filing past her, one by one, they accumulate the dawn.

No curtains on the windows, no eyelids to be closed. The welfare housing marches into view, purveying the climax of a century. Now you can watch the soaps in Japanese from six till noon. Now you can buy American, buy the world.

In the Happiness Department we are slaves, of our pain as of our praise. Here are tears of the visible...the invisible...

Pearls from the Magdalen.

3 HER LITANY

He promised you the love beyond all love: no difference, night or day: the eye of the storm, where motion dies: the roughness of his touch, where you kneel down to unbind the gift of tears. The lover is the knife inside the knife. He is the figure at twilight by the well, whose face you cannot see: Welcome, roots and briars have been placed across your path: the secret ferns, the mosses underfoot that only daybreak will reveal. At dawn he is the gardener, planting seeds beside the tomb. Here is the relinquishment, the blade: the filaments of light that speak in tongues: the turbulence on Monday in the park, your father sailing clear of all his pain: your mother, not a word: the moisture on the glass. These are loves: and will scar you till you heal, beyond the cautions of the world. Here or there, you will not know. Your name will be forgotten, like the dust on country roads. The wound was all you were, the wound that closes and keeps silent like a stone.

4 REFRAIN

Our sins are too weak to drink the rain. It beats us down, hard and unsought, fanning out along the bays and sandy coves. Beyond the beachheads and peninsulas: it lashes at our backs, whirling like a mirror on the sea.

The shipwreck goes unnoticed, the splinters die like sparks. A commonplace, the commonplace.

The wind has gathered them up, and they scatter "as though they had once been ourselves," points of light diminishing, receding from the many to the one.

This singing before any voice, free of possibility.

Nothing falters. Nothing also falters.

THE SERMON ON THE AIR

The heat of love is like a body we have added to our own: moist against the mirror, it hovers on the air. World and not of this world, neither place nor event. This clearing has no center, it ripples through the woods tree by tree. The timber-line unravels, the forest merging upward with the cliffs; above them an island of snow juts through the ocean of mist.

Still it is only a mask over mild, imperturbable eyes: the bareness, before we were sheltered. Kindly he laid his head to one side and observed us, smiling. His touch was in the residue of things, "our lives and our loves"; the chance design, pulsing for a second on the screen; the accidents, the plan; the bones and breath.

Slowness seeps from their wait in the light of day, the feathers of owls, the trillion wings of the insects, heavy with dew. Water drowses humbly in the shallows of the earth. How to say—not of fire nor of cloud, a pillar of comfort ascends and branches to heaven, roofing the nearness of night with its murmurous leaves.

If love is all you want, lean down, come here. A shining streams through the blood, like banners that float in the wind. Though all this time, our reflections hang suspended on the wall, to capture every movement and redeem; and will become us in the end...gravely and tenderly amused.—"You think you'll ever see him again?" "I reckon."

This morning she got the chicks she ordered from the Gospel Hour. Now she rocks herself awhile on the quiet porch, studying the county road. The radio dial is set to eight sixteen; pretty soon there'll be a sermon on the air. Dimly lit by the afterglow of sun, the dust settles lower in the fields. A bird sings three notes, like laughter from the middle of a dream. . .

But this we will never know until we are told.

PARADISE

After the film about some people I might have met, the evening had finally cleared. Fragile as glass, I walked around the neighborhood, careful to avoid being seen. I have never felt lonely, then or now—in my hours without order or direction, without regrets. But after the plays and novels and letters and all the casual talk every one of the thousands of days, I realized again: I have a life, I also have a life. It could never be deserved or explained away, it was there, there more stubbornly than any scrap of meaning, any gleam of clarity. Each of my friendships, each of my loves was like a stone in that hardened, windless solitude. Not a question of need but of the absolutely singular, the way you looked at me today when I held you by the hair and rocked you back and forth until you smiled. That was only once; once, as it had to be; in this moment, the child I call my own. My hand reaches down into the water, and the water overflows. You have a life, you also have a life.

But yours is easier to know than mine. It rests here before me like a table, a paragraph, an outpost of the mind. Thank God I can relive you as an axis far from suffering, emptily peripheral, a long vacation in the world. No quotient for that art has yet been found, though the parallels are endless. The whiteness of the shore, a naked page. The palms raving wildly in the wind, insane with the glitter from their fronds. But suddenly they stop, as though to listen...shallow roots still anchored lightly to the earth. Or again, the eclipse: a pyramid of twilight, weightlessly descending from a distance which our bodies misconceive. As day recedes, the birds twitter drowsily, bewildered by their laws. Minutes later, the sun will surprise them. The fact is not theirs, nor is it ours. As we think of them, we are equally unaware that we are equally... Forget about returning where you were. In the motion of the lines as they unroll is the passing of our lives, which could never have been said in just so many words, or just so few.

I remember, as though it were now: how afterwards you asked, "What is 'paraiso'?" "Paradise," I answered. The shifting stairs lose track of all our differences. We shed them like the breaths we will have shed within a year; and now, like a single breath. The physical body of meaning returns through the mirrors—a presence again, a survival. The cliffs are reflected in the lake, more solid in water than in air, brighter at sundown than by day. Above them are the clouds which tower like a summons here below, shining on our surface with a polish more durable than rock: world without end, without finality. It is the fox that sidled by across the tongue of silver sand, no sooner seen than lost forever; and the other one—identical—that follows seconds after. This is just the view from where we stand. The changes occur all at once, repeat after me. The opening is closing in on us, the closing is an opening. "I love you" makes sense for a moment. These are the marvels that keep us alive.

Again, the weather lifted. Most of this will still remain unsaid, subsiding in a wake of afterthoughts; our daily bread that crumbles hour by hour. The steps without return, the blades of grass have rehearsed it all before, the streams touched and entered by the tendrils of these mountains. For us and us alone, night awakens the flow through tousled banks, slows the blood to even measures in our veins. Soundlessly, our syllables persist, a glimmering that hovers at the confines of our sleep... We live where only dreams start and stir. . . All the ancient children are knowable in you, all their sly, cruel, harmless little games. Their bruises reappear on your face like the markings on a moth; the eyebrows and the hairline, the soft, golden down around the mouth, brush by me in the dark. I have to wonder, why we were allowed to come this close. For you, every question is an answer. Here is the night, not of our making. Here is the moon. Here are our bodies, the shadows of light.

RECESSIONAL

I

The branches of the tree lose their leaves as though the light were a blaze, the quietness a storm. Oblivious, the avalanche of time is passing over us, its cylinders perfected and unreal. To know us, then, preserved in the endlessly deflowering, the day.

Not for resurrection have we asked, but only to recall ourselves before the pictures fade. The rising is too simple: we stand, begin to walk and then to run. Our clothes are burned away in that motion—our habits and our names. But first we will remember the saying of ourselves, the words before a silence.

The hymn is still unfinished when the mind gazes only at itself, a mirror of corrections. Pain teaches us at first to be severe. But once we tame our hearts, the beast uncurls a long, spotted tail in the breeze of pleasure. The sails tug at their cords, the anchor is carelessly lifted.

This is the map, the writing on the wall. The sun looks tired, pinched and drawn; but the others have not noticed. We will always find them standing at their doors, dull and listless as before. Darkness has flooded their houses up to the roof. From our night we see it so; from our night, we see it clearly.

A hurricane churned inland through the hills; the river beds were altered. Boulders still keep watch among the ruins of the town. Steel or granite, cloth or bone, their shadows fill them out like a coloring: the dust through which they crumble into shadow, into dust, the powder and polish of all our borrowed things.

2

That grace, which you rested on us then, as on a meal that you would eat. And the graces who revisited the grove: the interlacing of their dance has rustled through the grass, each step has left a violet. Shyly they have sprung beside the stairs, the bridge of the inimitable...

All idols are the only one; if not, they would not be among the treasures that are here. Insatiable, insatiable, we try to own a spurious love. Song and wall and cloud and how are you and call me some other time. Then we do away with them, the inimitable.

The clumps of moss, the grease spots on the shade, the particles of soot that drizzle on the sill, seem to trace a threadbare sanctity—a pattern in the thinning threads of rain. Flickering the shorthand of retreat, the writing on the wall.

Because, and the becauses rub away from age to age, we decided to prolong this humble scene with all our wills, we may as well prolong it into the indefinite... Not what I make of you, or you of me, but what is made of us: the light which is always final, always a friend.

Begging to live in the body, but calling it the spirit, a colony of heaven. Proving that x equals y, trudging down the tunnel of an equal sign, year after year. Theory of the supernumeraries, theory of abundance, theory of the living. Theory of the evidence.

Of the faces I have worn—past, and passing, and to come—I think all three fit the best. This evening chill only sharpens the burden of distinction. At dawn the stones roll back, the wishful angels disappear. The clarity of witness—simply seeing-stumbles headlong through the heart.

3

How many blows can you take? How many screws? The winner takes them all; the only secret is that all the players win. But of that magic, and the smile which you administer before the end, as though you were saying: the light is come. Beyond that there must be a delighted murmur.

Everything is nothing but a style, and I foresee there will be nothing but the surge and the unraveling. They triumph from afar, the painted trumpets and imaginary palms, allowing you a wide remove in time or place. The anthem of the choir is as you are, in any act: naked and revealed; in any thought.

We came to love the sagging shelves, and the rust that trims the gate; the patient mildew and the moths; the useless praise of useless things. That was all the reason why we came. The daze of fortune weighs us down, and we have to be reminded in the passageways and halls. Through our fault, through our fault; most grievous.

The certainty awaits us like a predator its prey. Before we know, in the solitary room, we are hoping with imperfection instead of against it. The mirror hangs there as before: the bed, the floor, nothing has changed. But suddenly we are spectators, looking beyond ourselves, who hear without an echo: it is over.

The trick you performed was just a joke, as if to translate with a single sleight of hand all my blood and body into nothing. I was breathing with the air and as the air, draining away in the laughter. A trunk, a sword, a saw. Presto: empty space... So much for love. That is why I thank you, as long as we are here.

THE WINDOW

The light from the window is unfinished even now, breathing through the house like a second morning.

There it was: "the little death," the bond of pleasure. A thousand fadings to the west, a thousand awkward silences. The clumsy hand pressed down on the struggling mouth, struggling ever so slightly. Rehearsals for the bride, her chain, her veil.

The pearling fever of the world, the seeds of sweat that drop to earth. The wedding gifts, lost as if by accident. The child far below, turning slowly with his kite. His body as it turns with the wind.

The stars above the bay on a moonless night, the night on fire with—no, not them. The shadows then, the moon. The sun, the cloud. But no, you have to learn to crave specific things.

She stood at the corner for years, always the same, begging with her eyes that will never close.

The plant below the sill, erect in the holy light.

Our seeing changes us, but cannot change the world: this is the affliction, the cruelty of grace.

The heaving of that storm had swept their bodies overboard; they shone as one in the lightning like a scripture, the binding of a testament. It was the loss, not of innocence, but even of the faith that innocence exists. Beyond the ruin of the will the irreducible, the soul, turns away from us: and in the end, it is not ours. It governs with the guiding stars, ablaze at the helm of night, the blinded stars that dominate the sea. Below them is the shipwreck, the unburdening, the mast that topples forward, the sails torn and twisted on the reef.

Removed from us...removed with us.

The memory grows more distant. But I know it was a beach far to the north, a fin of the fish-shaped island. I remember the marvel of stripping off my clothes and plunging into the surf, the heavy, tumbling heartbeat. And swimming as hard as I could without losing a stroke, but being tossed into the air on the crest of every wave, tipped to one side and vaulted to weightlessness, to freedom. The presence of the world itself surged in on every swell, the life of all creatures rolling with me in the sway, the blankness of the foam leaping up, final every time, final.

ABOUT THE TYPEFACE

Bembo is a serif typeface created by the British branch of the Monotype Corporation in 1928–1929 and most commonly used for body text. It is a member of the 'old-style' of serif fonts, with its regular or roman style based on a design cut around 1495 by Francesco Griffo for Venetian printer Aldus Manutius, sometimes generically called the 'Aldine roman.' Bembo is named for Manutius's first publication with it, a small 1496 book by the poet and cleric Pietro Bembo. The italic is based on work by Giovanni Antonio Tagliente, a calligrapher who worked as a printer in the 1520s, after the time of Manutius and Griffo.

www.ingramcontent.com/pod-product-compliance
Lightning Source LLC
Chambersburg PA
CBHW020758130626
46554CB00006B/2250